St. John Lutheran Church (Ardrossan)
52233 Range Road

E 1C9

George is fighting
the fiery dragon.

D0394799

Contents

Acknowledgments
We have made every effort to trace copyright owners, and if we have omitted any necessary acknowledgments, we shall be happy to correct this in the next edition. For permission to include copyright material, we are grateful to The National Christian Education Council, for 'Down the air', 'Father, we thank Thee for the night', 'God, Who made the earth', 'God, Whose name is Love', 'Little bird, I have heard', 'Sing a song of springtime' and 'Tell me the stories of Jesus'; and to The Society for Promoting Christian Knowledge, for 'For butterflies and bees' and 'God always listens'.
The photographs on the endpapers were taken at Barwell Infants School, Leicestershire.

© LADYBIRD BOOKS LTD MCMLXXIX

Hymns and Songs

illustrated by DAVID PALMER

Ladybird Books Loughborough

All things bright and beautiful

All things bright and beautiful,
All creatures great and small,
All things wise and wonderful,
The Lord God made them all.

He gave us eyes to see them,
And lips that we might tell
How great is God Almighty
Who hath made all things well.

ALL THINGS BRIGHT AND BEAUTIFUL.   W. H. Monk.
1st Verse and refrain.

All things bright and beau - ti - ful,

All creatures great and small, All things wise and

won - der-ful, The Lord God made them all.

He gave us eyes to see them,

And lips that we might tell How great is God Al-

- migh - ty Who hath made all things well.

Away in a manger

Away in a manger,
No crib for a bed,
The little Lord Jesus
Laid down His sweet head.
The stars in the bright sky
Looked down where He lay,
The little Lord Jesus
Asleep on the hay.

CRADLE SONG.   W. J. Kirkpatrick.

A - way in a__ man-ger, no__ crib for a bed, The__ lit - tle Lord Je - sus laid__ down his sweet head. The stars in the__ bright sky looked down where He lay, The__ lit - tle Lord Je-sus a - sleep on the hay.

7

Harvest

When the corn is planted
In the deep dark bed,
Mothers know their children
Will have daily bread.

God sends sun and showers,
Birds sing overhead,
While the corn is growing
For our daily bread.

When the corn is gathered,
Stored in barn and shed,
Then we all are thankful
For our daily bread.

Father high in heaven,
All by Thee are fed;
Hear Thy children praise Thee
For our daily bread.

ST. CONSTANTINE.   W. H. Monk.

When   the   corn   is   plant - ed

In   the deep dark bed,   Mo-thers know their

chil - dren   Will have dai - ly   bread.

Down the air

Down the air
Everywhere
God is sending rain,
Dropping, dropping,
Dropping, dropping,
Down the window pane.
Pitter, patter,
Pitter, patter,
Down the window pane.
Pitter, patter,
Pitter, patter,
Thank God for the rain.

CHRISTMAS HYMN.   Welsh traditional.

Down the air   ev - 'rywhere   God is send-ing

rain,   Dropping, dropping, dropping, dropping,

Down the win-dow pane.   Pit - ter, pat - ter,

pit - ter, pat - ter, Down the win-dow pane,

Pit - ter,   pat - ter,   pit - ter,   pat - ter,

Thank God   for   the   rain.

11

Father, we thank Thee for the night

Father, we thank Thee for the night,
And for the pleasant morning light,
For rest and food, and loving care,
And all that makes the day so fair.
Help us to do the things we should,
To be to others kind and good,
In all we do, at work, or play,
To grow more loving every day.

SOLOTHURN.   Swiss Traditional Melody.

Fa - ther, we thank Thee for   the   night,

And   for the plea-sant morn - ing   light,

For   rest and food, and   lov - ing   care,

And   all that makes the   day   so   fair.

13

For butterflies and bees

For butterflies and bees,
For singing birds and trees,
For flowers and wind and sun,
We thank God, everyone.

For food, and clothes and fun,
For strength to walk and run,
For home, and school and friends,
Our song of thanks ascends.

ST. CECILIA.

L. G. Hayne.

For but - ter - flies and bees, For

singing birds and trees, For flowers and wind and

sun, We thank God, ev - ery - one.

Greeting

Come and let us sing,
Sing with happy voices,
For when we are glad,
God Himself rejoices.

He who gives the birds
All their merry singing,
To the boys and girls,
Oh, such joy is bringing.

Sing when days are dark,
Sing when rain is falling;
Clouds will soon be gone,
Birds will soon be calling.

Sing, then, all the way,
Sing a song of gladness;
Sing, then, every day,
Sing away the sadness.

GREETING.

Edwyn Vincent.

Come and let us sing, Sing with hap - py voi - ces, For when we are glad, God Him - self___ re - joi - ces.

God always listens

God always listens
Whenever we pray.
He's never too busy
To hear what we say.
So we will say, "Thank you"
For what each day brings,
Children to play with
And many good things.

GOD ALWAYS LISTENS.   F. Willson.

God al-ways lis-tens When-ev-er we pray.

He's nev-er too bu-sy To hear what we

say.   So   we will   say, "Thank you" For

what each day   brings,   Chil-dren to

play with And   ma-ny   good things.

God, Who made the earth

God, Who made the earth,
The air, the sky, the sea,
Who gave the light its birth,
Careth for me.

God, Who made the grass,
The flower, the fruit, the tree,
The day and night to pass,
Careth for me.

SOMMERLIED. H. Von Muller.

God, Who made the earth, The air, the sky, the
sea, Who gave the light its
birth, Car - eth for me.

God, Whose name is Love

God, Whose name is Love,
Happy children we,
Listen to the hymn
That we sing to Thee.

Help us to be good,
Always kind and true,
In the games we play
Or the work we do.

HASLEMERE.   Old Air.

God, Whose name is Love, Hap-py chil-dren we,

Lis-ten to the hymn That we sing to Thee.

Jesus bids us shine

Jesus bids us shine
With a pure, clear light,
Like a little candle
Burning in the night.
In this world is darkness
We must shine,
You in your small corner
And I in mine.

Jesus bids us shine, then
For all around.
Many kinds of darkness
In this world are found.
Sin, and want, and sorrow,
So we must shine,
You in your small corner
And I in mine.

JESUS BIDS US SHINE

E. O. Excell.

Je-sus bids us shine With a pure, clear light,

Like a lit-tle can-dle Burn-ing in the night.

In this world is dark-ness We_ must shine,

You in your small cor-ner And I in mine.

Heavenly Father,
hear my prayer

Heavenly Father, hear my prayer:
Night and day I'm in Thy care;
Look upon me from above,
Bless the home I dearly love;
Bless the friends with whom I play,
Make us kinder day by day.

CROWLAND.   J. Schop.

Heaven-ly   Fa - ther,   hear   my   prayer:

Night   and   day   I'm   in   Thy   care;

Look   up - on   me   from   a - bove,

Bless the home I dear - ly love;

Bless the friends with whom I play,

Make us kind - er day by day.

Jesus loves me, this I know

Jesus loves me, this I know,
For the Bible tells me so.
Little ones to Him belong,
They are weak, but He is strong.
Yes, Jesus loves me,
Yes, Jesus loves me,
Yes, Jesus loves me,
The Bible tells me so.

Boys and girls across the sea,
Jesus loves, as well as me,
So our little friends are they
And with us they all can say,
"Yes, Jesus loves me,
Yes, Jesus loves me,
Yes, Jesus loves me,
The Bible tells me so."

JESUS LOVES ME.   W. B. Bradbury.

Je-sus loves me, this I know, For the Bi - ble

tells me so.   Lit - tle ones to   Him be-long,

They are weak, but He   is strong. Yes,   Je - sus

loves me,   Yes,   Je-sus loves me,   Yes, Je-sus

loves me,   the   Bi - ble tells me   so.

Little bird, I have heard

Little bird, I have heard
What a merry song you sing,
Soaring high to the sky
On your tiny wing.

GERMAN AIR.

Lit - tle bird, I have heard What a mer - ry

song you sing, Soar-ing high to the sky

On your ti - ny wing. Jesu's lit - tle

lambs are we, And He loves us, you and me,

As we share in His care We must hap-py be.

Jesu's little lambs are we,
And He loves us, you and me,
As we share in His care
We must happy be.

All the day, lambs at play
In the fields where daisies grow,
Skip about, in and out,
They are happy so.

Now the day is over

Now the day is over,
Night is drawing nigh,
Shadows of the evening
Steal across the sky.

Now the darkness gathers,
Stars begin to peep,
Birds and beasts and flowers
Soon will be asleep.

EUDOXIA.   S. Baring-Gould.

Now the day is ov - er, Night is draw-ing nigh,

Shadows of the even-ing Steal a-cross the sky.

33

Once in royal David's city

Once in royal David's city,
Stood a lowly cattle shed,
Where a mother laid her baby,
In a manger for His bed.
Mary was that mother mild,
Jesus Christ her little child.

He came down to earth
                    from heaven,
Who is God and Lord of all,
And His shelter was a stable,
And His cradle was a stall.
With the poor, and meek
                    and lowly,
Lived on earth our Saviour holy.

IRBY.   H. J. Gauntlett.

Once in roy - al Da - vid's ci - ty,

Stood a low - ly cat - tle shed,

Where a mo - ther laid her_ ba by,

In a man - ger for_ His_ bed.

Ma - ry was that mo - ther mild,

Je - sus Christ her lit - tle child.

Praise Him, praise Him

Praise Him, praise Him,
All ye little children,
He is love, He is love.
Praise Him, praise Him
All ye little children,
He is love, He is love.

Thank Him, thank Him,
All ye little children,
He is love, He is love.
Thank Him, thank Him,
All ye little children,
He is love, He is love.

PRAISE HIM.   E. R. Bailey.

Praise Him, praise Him,   All ye lit-tle chil-dren

He   is   love,   He   is   love.

Praise Him, praise Him, All ye lit-tle chil-dren

He is love, He is love.

Twinkle, twinkle, little star

Twinkle, twinkle, little star,
How I wonder what you are,
Up above the world so high,
Like a diamond in the sky.
Twinkle, twinkle, little star,
How I wonder what you·are.

NURSERY TUNE.

Twin - kle, twin - kle, lit - tle star,

How I won - der what you are,

Up a - bove the world so high,

Like a dia - mond in the sky.

Twin - kle, twin - kle, lit - tle star,

How I won - der what you are.

39

When lamps are lighted
in the town

When lamps are lighted
                 in the town,
The boats sail out to sea.
The fishers watch when
                 night comes down,
They work for you and me.
We little children go to rest.
Before we sleep, we pray
That God will bless the fishermen
And bring them back at day.

BALLERMA.   F. H. Barthelemon.

When lamps are light - ed   in   the town, The

boats   sail   out_   to   sea. ____   The

fish - ers watch when night comes down, They

work_   for   you ___   and   me. _____

41

Sing a song of springtime

Sing a song of springtime,
Sing a song of spring.
Flowers are in their beauty,
Birds are on the wing.
Springtime, springtime,
God has given us springtime.
Thank Him for His gift of love,
Thank Him for the spring.

MAY TIME.

W. G. Hancock.

Sing a song of spring-time, Sing a song of

spring, __ Flowers are in their beau - ty,

Birds are on the wing. Spring-time, spring-time,

God has given us spring-time, Thank Him for His

gift of love, Thank Him for the spring.

43

Tell me the stories of Jesus

Tell me the stories of Jesus
I love to hear.
Things I would ask Him to tell me
If He were here.
Scenes by the wayside,
Tales of the sea,
Stories of Jesus,
Tell them to me.

STORIES OF JESUS.

F. A. Challinor.

Tell me the sto-ries of Je - sus I love to hear. Things I would ask Him to tell me If He were here. Scenes by the

way - side, Tales of the sea,___ Sto - ries of

Je - sus, Tell them to me.___

Sunny bank

As I sat on a sunny bank,
On Christmas Day in the morning—

I spied three ships come sailing by,
On Christmas Day in the morning.

And who should be with
                    those three ships,
But Joseph and his fair lady!

O he did whistle, and she did sing,
On Christmas Day in the morning.

And all the bells on earth did ring,
On Christmas Day in the morning.

For joy that our Saviour
　　　　　　　　　he was born,
On Christmas Day in the morning.

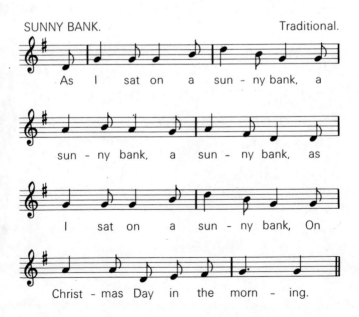

SUNNY BANK.　　　　　　　　　Traditional.

As I sat on a sun - ny bank, a
sun - ny bank, a sun - ny bank, as
I sat on a sun - ny bank, On
Christ - mas Day in the morn - ing.

We plough the fields and scatter

We plough the fields and scatter
The good seed on the land,
But it is fed and watered
By God's almighty hand.
He sends the snow in winter,
The warmth to swell the grain,
The breezes and the sunshine
And soft, refreshing rain.

All good gifts around us
Are sent from Heaven above,
Then thank the Lord
O thank the Lord
For all His love.

WIR PFLÜGEN.   J. A. P. Schule.

We plough the fields and scat - ter The good seed on the land, But it is fed and wa - tered By God's al - migh-ty hand.

He sends the snow in win - ter, The warmth to swell the grain, The breez-es and the sun - shine And soft, re-fresh-ing rain.

All good gifts a - round us Are sent from heaven a - bove, Then thank the Lord O thank the Lord For all___ His love.

Thank you for the world so sweet

Thank you for the world so sweet;
Thank you for the food we eat;
Thank you for the birds that sing:
Thank you, God, for everything!

BATTISHILL.   J. Battishill.

Thank you for the world so sweet;

Thank you for the food we eat;

Thank you for the birds that sing;

Thank you, God, for ev - ery - thing!